Judo

First published in 2011
by Wayland

Copyright © Wayland 2011

Wayland
338 Euston Road
London NW1 3BH

Wayland Australia
Level 17/207 Kent Street
Sydney, NSW 2000

Series Editor: Louise John
Editor: Katie Woolley
Design: D.R.ink
Consultant: Shirley Bickler
Photographer: Andy Crawford

A CIP catalogue record for this book is available
from the British Library.

ISBN 9780750264969

Printed in China

Wayland is a division of Hachette Children's Books,
an Hachette UK Company

www.hachette.co.uk

The Publisher and author would like to thank all of the models who took part in this book.

Contents

Judo club

My name is Lily and I am six. I have just started going to judo classes after school.

Getting ready

My judo class is held every Friday for an hour. I wear my judo jacket, trousers and belt.

My hair is tied back and I have bare feet.

The Dojo

My judo class is held in the school gym.

We call our judo hall the Dojo.
It has mats on the floor.

My sisters

I say hello to my sisters, Ellie and Grace. We all do judo together. We wear white belts because we are beginners.

We train with a partner. Today Ellie is going to be my partner.

The warm-up

We always start with a warm-up game.
This game is called "Mirrors".

We stand on the mats and copy the teacher. This helps us to practise our balance and footwork.

Top Tips

The warm-up prepares the mind and body for judo.

Throws

Next we practise our throws. There are lots of different throws to learn in judo.

When I do the throw well, Ellie will
lose her balance and fall down.

Break-falls

We have to learn how to fall and land safely on the mat. Tom shows us how to do this.

Then I have a go! This is called doing a break-fall.

Top Tips

It is important to keep your head tucked in as you fall.

Taking a break

We stop to have a break and drink some water.

Top Tips

It is important to drink plenty of water when you exercise.

Then Tom shows us the hold
we are going to practise today.
It is called a chest hold.

chest holds

I have to hold Ellie down on the mat.
Then Ellie practises the chest hold on me.

Tom comes round to help us get
the hold right.

Mini matches

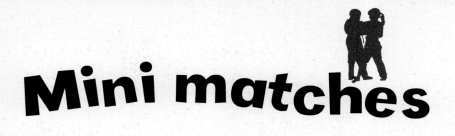

Near the end of the lesson
we have a mini match.
We all bow to our partners.

Tom watches us to see how we do our
throws and holds.

Who will win?

We win a match by getting points.
We get points for a good throw or hold.

Top Tips

In judo, you can win a match with a perfect throw.

I am pleased because today I win
my match against Ellie!

Dead Ants!

We finish the lesson by playing a game called "Dead Ants".

Tom calls out "dead ants!". We all
have to lie down like a dead ant
and the last one to do so is out!

Going home

At the end of the lesson, we all bow as we leave the Dojo.

It is time to go home. Dad has come to pick me and my sisters up.

I can't wait for judo next week!

START READING is a series of highly enjoyable books for beginner readers. **The books have been carefully graded to match the Book Bands widely used in schools.** This enables readers to be sure they choose books that match their own reading ability.

Look out for the Band colour on the book in our Start Reading logo.

The Bands are:

	Pink Band 1A & 1B
	Red Band 2
	Yellow Band 3
	Blue Band 4
	Green Band 5
	Orange Band 6
	Turquoise Band 7
	Purple Band 8
	Gold Band 9

START READING books can be read independently or shared with an adult. They promote the enjoyment of reading through satisfying stories, plays and non-fiction narratives, which are supported by fun illustrations and photographs.

Jillian Powell has written many fiction and non-fiction books for children. She began writing stories when she was just four years old and she hasn't stopped since! She lives in a house beside a village church and still sits down to write every day.